STARTING TO SAIL

T. Ladd

STARTING TO SAIL

written and illustrated by
DAVID COBB, R.O.I.

LONDON   ILIFFE BOOKS LTD

First published in 1964 for
YACHTING WORLD by Iliffe Books Ltd
Dorset House, Stamford Street, London, S.E.1

Printed and bound in England by
The Chapel River Press Ltd.
Andover, Hants.
BKS 5033

CONTENTS

FOREWORD

The day of the lone amateur sailor, bumbling away happily in blissful ignorance, is drawing to a close. All the pressures of advertising and the press are busy seeing to that. This creeping barrage of advice and ideas, fortified by reports of majestic cruises and colossal racing fleets, tends to obscure the simpler facts of sailing life. The first of these is that anybody who can afford say £40–£50 can buy a good second-hand sailing dinghy. The second is that in a few days of suitable weather, in sheltered surroundings, he can learn to sail it.

No book will replace a good instructor, and while crewing for someone else teaches one much about crewing, it still doesn't teach one to sail. Nothing concentrates the mind so much as being responsible for one's own boat.

It is not possible for the newcomer to foretell whether sailing is going to prove a satisfactory hobby, but if a liking for fresh air and a physical challenge is linked with an independent outlook, boats should be a success. If he has any idea of keeping a boat merely to impress other people, then it won't last long, and there is no need to read any more.

The manner and sequence in which I have approached the subject may be regarded by some as heretical; but in order to detect and denounce heresy you have already to be expert and orthodox. So this book is not for you either. This is for those families, for instance, which have been swept afloat by zealous and experienced sailing husbands without a chance first to do their own kindergarten sailing, and for the true beginner.

Brockenhurst, 1964   DAVID COBB

To Jean and Mairet, in love and gratitude for the happiness they have brought, and found, afloat.

Chapter 1

CHOICE OF BOAT

ONE reason for writing about choosing a boat is that today this field of choice is of such heroic size. Fifty years ago, or even thirty, a sailing dinghy was just a sailing dinghy. Probably it started life as a tender to a fair-sized yacht, had nice lines, rowed well and sailed indifferently. It was well built in a rather heavy traditional way, and spent most of its life tied up on a hard or to a jetty. If anyone had suggested lifting it on to a trailer to drive 50 miles to the coast for a weekend sail, surprise would have burst its kapok fender.

This sort of dinghy is built less often today, but it has many solid virtues. It is usually stable because of its weight, and it will stand a lot of hard wear and tear; the scars it suffers are mostly superficial. Because of its dual role of sailing and rowing it usually carries a simple and not very efficient rig, but it will be a mistake to dismiss such a type simply because it does not sail as effectively as a modern dinghy designed solely for that purpose. The inherent stability means less bother about keeping the boat upright by 'sitting it out', and the simple rig means short spars and the minimum of rigging. The low-pressure performance gives more time to think than do the ejector-seat antics required by a performance dinghy, and when the inevitable come-alongside occurs with too much speed, the robust structure will shrug off a bump without concern. Ideally this type of boat should be kept at the waterside in such a manner that it floats each tide, for prolonged periods hauled out in hot summer weather tend to dry out the planking and cause leaks.

If this problem of getting afloat can be solved only by trailing a boat to the sea, then obviously the weight factor matters; and while I regard the modern light-construction dinghy as rather less suitable for a beginner, then, perforce, that must be the choice. This boat may be any one of numerous standard designs, such as the Heron, Cadet, Scow 'Y.W.' G.P. 14, and so on. The marginal differences between them count for little at this stage, provided the buyer first assures himself by a little comparative research that he is paying no more than he should.

It is quite likely that the beginner will have made his first ventures afloat in a sailing school, and an excellent idea this is, for by the time he feels ready for his own boat he will have heard discussed and seen used at least one, and possibly several, other types. In this case he will draw on some of the experience he has gained to make a choice.

Other factors which must be foreseen are precisely what this boat is meant to do, as well as float and sail. So far we have considered the crew/owner as being one person. People being what they are, this situation will not last long— soon there will be somebody else, a friend whose company adds much to the enjoyment, but he/she takes up space. This must be allowed for. Again there may be some local class, not necessarily which races, but which is fitted in some particular respect to the district where it lives. It may well be worth considering one of these, for its ownership automatically confers a degree of fellowship with a number of other people, which can hardly fail to be a help.

The success of joining a club in the hope of learning more

Lymington Scow

'Yachting World' Heron

Traditional type

Fairey Duckling

quickly how to sail is such a personal decision that it is hardly possible to define its usefulness to any particular person. Much will depend on the type of club, and its activities; and in any case a number of people go afloat with a half-formed and perhaps unadmitted idea of escaping from their fellow men for a few hours. On the other hand the facilities which clubs offer by way of landing stages and dinghy parking are immensely useful; and membership leads to an agreeable association with people of linked interests. Many clubs, as well as fostering activities afloat during the summer, have a programme of winter lectures which cover a wide range of sailing subjects.

Taking it, as we may with confidence, that there is no shortage of boats, there comes next the problem of new or second-hand, and whether to buy on the large or small side. My own choice would be for the large side, bought second-hand and for these reasons.

The larger boat (within reasonable limits; I mean 14 feet, not 14 tons) is less sensitive to minor errors of trim and helmsmanship and will give you a little more time to think. The behaviour of a very small, say 8 feet, sailing dinghy is highly volatile—a puff of wind needs instant counter-action, and even moving swiftly in a very small dinghy needs practice, leaving aside matters of steering and trim of sails. The extra size also means that other people can be aboard enjoying some freedom of movement.

I have on occasions met people who have launched forthwith into really large yachts, without any preamble, and while I admire their spirit, I think it essential to serve some short apprenticeship. A large yacht requires a crew, and it is unfair to anyone to ask them to ship aboard a vessel of say 15–25 tons whose owner knows little or nothing of how to handle her. If such an owner can shade his eyes from the

glamour of his forthcoming cruise (these ships are always bound for the Antipodes) and spare time to spend a month or so sailing small open boats, his chances of arrival will be greatly enhanced, and there will be harmony aboard his fine ship.

The argument in favour of buying second-hand, apart from the reduced outlay, is based on thinking it a mistake to acquire any brand new machine on which to learn; whether it is a car, aeroplane, or a billiard table. Obviously the learner is prone to misjudgement—and whether he bends the car, pancakes the 'plane, or cuts the cloth, his concern is likely to increase with the amount he has at stake. The upper limits of size and 'second-handness' in a boat are reached when (a) it is so large that the owner is frightened to get it under way for fear of losing control, and (b) when the age of a boat is such that it is no longer really sound, and bits start coming off. Common sense, and the services of a surveyor will deal respectively with these two matters.

On the other hand many people do not wish to start to sail a boat where somebody else has just left off. Assessing its condition and wondering whether they have bought badly are unwelcome and, in their view, unnecessary worries which are best removed forthwith by purchasing a new boat; few will dispute that view-point, so weigh these two arguments and make your choice.

In any case do not imagine that the boat you are about to buy will demand the same terms of permanent affection as, for instance, a wife, '. . . till death do you part'. Within a year or so, as confidence grows, so will your ideas, and with them will come the urge to own something a little larger, more capable, and better able to execute the particular type of sailing which you find is most to your taste.

At the end of it all there arises the question of money. Over the past 20 years a large area of newsprint has shown convincingly that it is no longer necessary to be a rich man in order to sail—quite so. The corollary which should receive equal publicity, but hasn't, is the error of thinking that the more money you spend on buying a boat, the more fun you will get out of it. The two matters are unrelated. Enjoyment cannot be bought, it is a state of mind; and you may find it in equal evidence, or absence, aboard anything from a battered 12 foot dinghy to a pristine International 12-metre Cup Challenger. It arises from the tonic effect of getting afloat into a world where all the normal bothers and exactions of life are gently but firmly replaced by enforced attention to the matters in hand, whether they be the way to put the tiller, the best means of getting off the mud bank you have just hit, that impressively beautiful sunset, or the novel effect of salt water in egg-and-tomato sandwiches. Having a rather grand boat, or a very ordinary one, is neither help nor hindrance to such mystical considerations.

At the end of it all you will have acquired something like this:

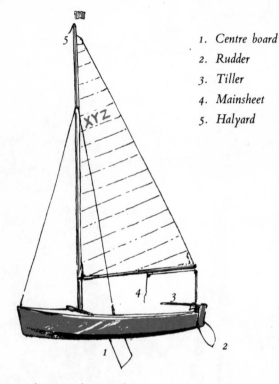

1. Centre board
2. Rudder
3. Tiller
4. Mainsheet
5. Halyard

To make it ready to sail:

1. Place the rudder in position.
2. Lower the centreboard.
3. Attach the halyard by its shackle to the yard, or sail.
4. Reeve the mainsheet (i.e. feed the end of it through the block on the boom, and tie a knot in the end).
5. Put the tiller into the rudder head.

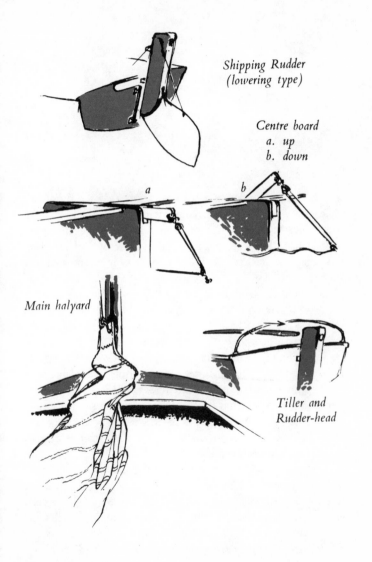

*Shipping Rudder
(lowering type)*

*Centre board
a. up
b. down*

a

b

Main halyard

*Tiller and
Rudder-head*

Chapter 2

SAILING—1

IT is only natural that books on sailing a boat should be written by those who have mastered the technique, but sometimes it seems that the more skilled as seamen the writers have become, the more difficult they find the non-technical expression of their ideas. In consequence the subject is invested often with a crop of definitions and glossaries fit to rig and run a Cape Horn windjammer.

Now a driving instructor does not lightly stun his new pupil by reciting the entire provisions of the Road Traffic Act 1960, followed by a brisk lecture on the design of a hypoid floating back-axle. No; for him it's enough to point out that pulled this way the steering wheel puts you in the ditch, and that way collides you head on with an oncoming Corporation bus—and to avoid these and similar setbacks all you need to do is to crawl slowly along, going serenely straight until you have the feel of the thing. In my view it should be much the same with a boat.

If you are teaching yourself, take the boat on a fine quiet day under oars to a non-tidal sheltered piece of water away from other moving craft; hitch it up to a post by the same sort of knot you habitually use to tie up the clothesline. Leave the bowline till later. Hoist the sail, lower the centre-board, hang the rudder on the stern, put in the tiller and see that the various ropes are all clear, then hold the mainsheet in your hand. Do *not* make it fast.

The very light breeze which scarcely ruffles the water (and that's the only sort of breeze we want) will be coming from ahead, because any dinghy hitched up by its painter will lie pointing towards the wind, and its sail will be flapping gently overhead from its mast exactly as a flag does from its flagpole.

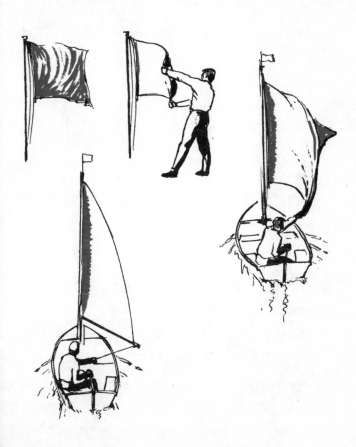

Pause for a minute and think about this flag and flagpole idea, and consider this breeze blowing gently across the water, always from the same direction. Wherever one places the flagpole and flag, if one catches the two free corners of the flag and pulls them to one side or the other, the flag ceases to flap, and the wind fills it into a smooth bulging square which pulls steadily at one's hands. It is precisely such a pull which is going to drive the boat along.

All that is needed to start the boat sailing is to unhitch the painter from the post and give the boat's bow a good push sideways so that she swings round until at right angles

to the wind. By the time you have got back to the tiller the sail will have stopped flapping and filled to a gentle curve, and the boat will be moving forwards. The two ends of the 'flag' have been pulled to one side, and in turn it is pulling the boat along.

The control of the 'flag' is conveniently arranged by a single rope, the mainsheet, and the only adjustment this needs is to be let out until the 'flag' shows the first signs of flapping on the edge next to the mast.

One or two very gentle exploratory to-and-fro movements
of the tiller will quickly show its effect in guiding the boat
and at this stage it is better to keep the course at right angles
to the wind by steering for a distant mark on the bank, and
steadying the dinghy's bow in line with it.   After a few

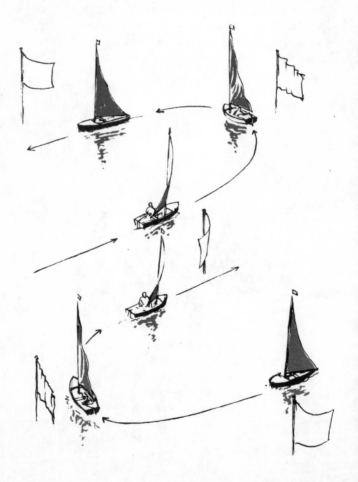

minutes it is time to turn round, and the easiest direction to turn at this early stage is by swinging the bow towards the wind, making the sail into a free-flapping 'flag' once more as the dinghy curves round. So push the tiller firmly away from the direction of the wind, and keep it there. The bite of the rudder on the passing water will force the stern in the same direction, and the bow will swing round towards the wind. Halfway round the boat will be pointing directly at the wind and the sail will have turned into a free-flapping 'flag' once more. This stage is called being *in stays*. As the swing of the boat continues, the pull of the mainsheet begins to drag the sail out of line with the breeze, the 'flag' fills with wind on the other side, the wrinkles disappear, the boat gathers way once more. Bring the tiller back to the centre position and settle the boat on her new course, directly back towards your starting post. At this early stage, whenever going about, it is well to develop the habit of changing from side to side of the boat, facing forward all the time. While it may be physically easier to swivel round the other way, facing the stern, many beginners find that in the process they lose touch with what is happening behind their back, and by the time they have got settled in the new tack, the boat has swung too far off the wind.

This simple exercise is known as sailing with a beam wind, or *reaching*, and at the end of the outward leg you have *gone about*. If at any time the breeze should strengthen a little, the pressure of the sail will heel the boat. This is nothing to be alarmed about; counterbalance the heel by moving a little across the boat towards the side on which the wind is blowing, or in proper parlance, the *windward* side. When the breeze eases off again, move back towards the *leeward* or lee side. In a puff of wind the tiller, which so far has needed barely any pressure, needs a little extra pull to windward in order to keep the boat on a straight course for the point selected as a mark. When back near the post, turn the dinghy round by exactly the same process, pushing the tiller towards the sail etc., except that it is done 'mirrorwise'. This gentle progress to and fro, on a nice sunny day, should give you the chance to get the feel of the tiller, and the pull of the mainsheet, but after an hour or so of reaching and going about it is only reasonable to think it time to stop, for a stand easy, before attempting something else.

This breeze which has been propelling the boat quietly to and fro has also the power to retard and finally halt her. All that is needed is to turn the bow of the boat towards the wind, and so convert the sail into a flapping 'flag' once more, robbed of its power to propel, when the boat will stop.

To return to tie up to the starting post, sail first towards a point a boat's length downwind or to leeward of it. Just before reaching that point, push the tiller firmly to leeward; the bow will swing quickly towards the post and the boat will curve round, bow to wind, losing speed as she does so, allowing you to grasp the post as it comes alongside. So far so good. In a beam wind you are master of your fate and captain of your soul. How about the other two major points of sailing, namely *beating* and *running*?

Beating (or *tacking*) is not very different from the reaching process just mastered, but whereas the boat has been sailing to and fro over the same stretch of water, there will come a time when you wish to sail to a point which lies somewhere to windward, perhaps directly upwind. Manifestly the boat must sail there; this is a sailing boat; it has no other way of getting there.

Cast off from the post in exactly the same manner as before.

Get the boat sailing and then slowly haul in the mainsheet until its pull flattens the sail. At the same time push the

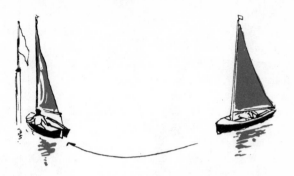

tiller gently a trifle to leeward, so that the bow of the boat swings progressively towards the wind. Oddly enough the flattened sail continues to drive the boat, even when it is pointing at quite a narrow angle towards the wind, but the moment the sail shows a tendency to flap (or become a free-flapping flag) due to the wind getting round behind it, that is the point to check her windward swing with a slight pull on the tiller. You are now beating, or as it is sometimes termed, *tacking close-hauled*, and while the boat is not heading precisely towards the goal, she is approaching it exactly in the zig-zag manner of the path which leads up a very steep hill, and for the same reason that a direct approach is impracticable.

After some moments heading in this direction (or on this 'tack') it will become clear that you are now as close to your new goal as you can get on this course. In fact quite soon the gap will start to widen. This is the moment to repeat precisely the process used at the end of each of the reaches—by pushing the tiller away from the wind, and turning the

bow round towards the wind to 'go about'. As the sail fills on the new tack, the objective lies nearly ahead, and in a few minutes it will be close aboard. You have learnt to beat or tack to windward.

Only one major point of sailing remains. It is running before the wind, or just *running*. To return to your starting point that is what you will need to do. By now your starting post is directly downwind, and to sail straight to it you have

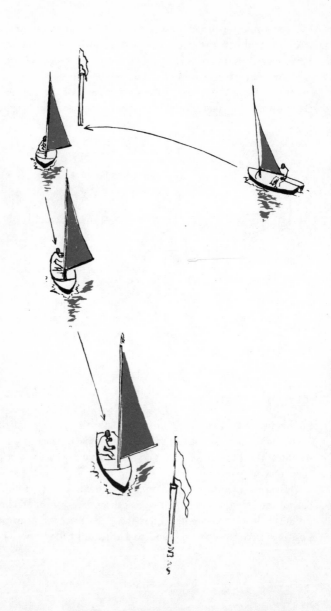

merely to let out the mainsheet to its full extent, so that the sail is nearly at right angles to the centreline of the boat, point the bow towards the post, and wait for the gentle wind to take you to it. You are running. You know how to sail—or do you?

Chapter 3

SAILING—2

THREE descriptions of progress—beating, reaching and running—contain the basis of sailing. They require the boat to be sailed with the wind striking one or other side of the bow, on the beam, or directly on the stern. But these categories, while descriptively convenient, divide in an artificial and inelastic way; one may wish to sail a little closer to the wind than reaching, and yet not be fully close hauled (called *a point free*). Again the dinghy may have the wind from a point halfway between the beam and the stern (a *quartering* wind). In the first case the mainsheet should be eased a little from the close hauled position; in the second it should be trimmed to keep the boom at right angles to the wind.

So far the wind has been described as if it was blowing steadily throughout, but in practice it will be found that minor changes in strength and direction occur all the time, particularly when trees, high banks or large craft lie close to windward. This means that one's eye must glance incessantly at the tell-tale burgee to detect and react to its variations. This is particularly important when running dead before the wind, with the boom and sail *broad off*, or at right angles to the centreline of the boat.

A moment's thought will show that at such times the sail

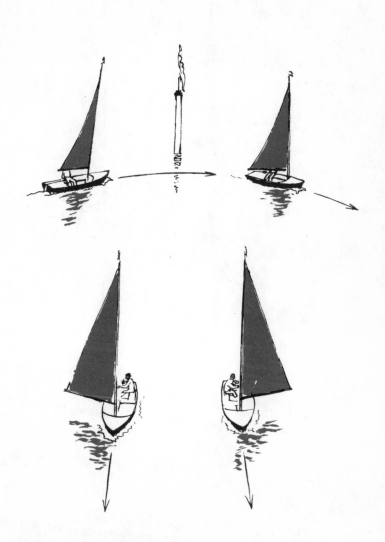

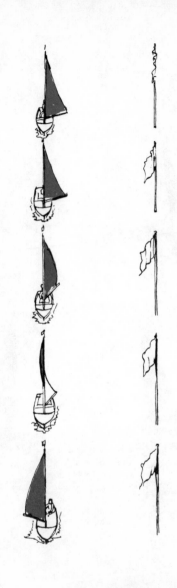

can be on either side with equally satisfactory results. The two positions are symmetrical.

However, if the wind begins to blow from slightly to one or other side of dead astern, the dinghy has now a windward and a leeward side even though the difference may not at first be very apparent to the helmsman, but from what we have already learned it is essential and natural for the sail always to be on the leeward side of the boat. If therefore, it is noted when running that the wind is tending to blow even slightly from the same side as the sail (making it the windward side) it becomes important to pass the sail across to leeward. This is known as a *gybe*, and it comes in two models, intentional and unintentional.

The intentional *gybe* is enacted by maintaining the course of the dinghy, and hauling in the mainsheet steadily and firmly, meanwhile keeping a keen eye on the sail. When the boom end is approaching the stern, the wind will finally strike the far side of the sail, and whisk it smartly across the boat. It is essential to be ready and watchful for this occurrence, and the second it takes place *to allow the mainsheet to run out to its full extent.* Some slight counterbalancing may be necessary, by shifting one's weight across to the windward side, but the vital factor is the released mainsheet. If, in a breeze, the sheet is allowed to catch up, pinning the sail in a close-hauled position, a capsize is difficult to avert, and this is the reason for guarding against an unintentional *gybe*. Such an event occurs as a surprise, and one is unprepared mentally and physically for the speedy reactions which are needed.

However, in the light breeze which we require for these early lessons, an unintentional *gybe* will result in, if anything, no more than a smart tap on the head as the boom goes over, but to practice the intentional manoeuvre, select a clear down-wind stretch of some length, and run down it with the wind aft, curving in a series of slow S-bends, gybing each time the wind begins to blow from the same side as the sail. Very soon the feel of the manoeuvre will become familiar.

There is another method, when running, of shifting the mainsail from one side of the boat to the other, and while its usefulness is not apparent in conditions of light to moderate winds, there will come a moment later on when it is a very present help in time of trouble.

The dinghy is running fast before the fresh breeze, and little wave crests are chasing along astern of her. There is rather a lot of wind, even going away before it, and the many other boats under way distract one's attention. Quite suddenly there comes a peculiar feeling of lightness in the

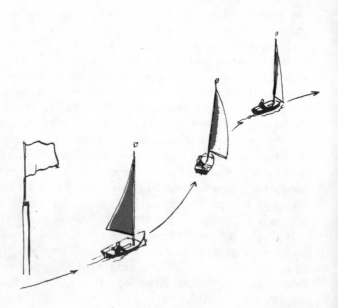

pull of the tiller, and the boom-end starts to lift. Nothing tangible is wrong, merely you feel as you might if there was a twist in your braces. The dinghy, you realise at last, is running by the lee, on the edge of an unintentional gybe, and the prospect of that sail, however it comes, slamming across, is distinctly worrying. Desist. There is a different and entirely armchair escape from this dilemma.

Instead of hauling in the mainsheet, push the tiller gently towards the sail. Under the influence of the slight angle of the rudder the course of the dinghy curves round until the wind is blowing from directly astern. Keep the tiller in the same position, and slowly the dinghy continues to curve its course round, causing the wind direction to strike next the quarter (when you move up to windward), then the beam, and finally the dinghy has turned so far round that the wind is now beginning to strike the bow, and to keep her sailing you haul in the mainsheet until taut, so that she is beating to windward. As soon as she is moving well, put her about, on to the other tack, but instead of continuing close-hauled, bear away steadily, paying out the mainsheet steadily at the same time. In a few seconds she is back on to the original course, running sweetly and swiftly with the sail comfortably full, and the wind now clearly on the weather quarter. But what is this? the boom is now on the opposite side—

we've gybed? No, but in effect we have, and that is what we
wanted to do.

For fear of complicating something I may have made clear,
I won't analyse this phenomenon except to point out that
instead of gybing by maintaining the dinghy's course and
hauling the sail bodily by the mainsheet towards the wind,
until it blew on the opposite side and slammed the boom
across, the sail from a broad off position has been allowed to

swing away from the wind, through the stage where it
became a flapping flag (when going about) and has finally
been pulled out to the broad off position on the opposite
side. It has been allowed to pivot freely to leeward round
the mast, while the dinghy has been steered in a complete
circle underneath.

Rather than leave this manoeuvre until it is urgently necessary, follow the gybing practice with a few circuits of this type to become familiar with the initially rather confusing business of turning circles under sail—not that the matter is in any way difficult when one faces forward all the time and concentrates on the sail and the burgee, rather than on the rapidly swinging shoreline.   Only after the evolutions described so far are completely familiar, has the time come to explore a little further afield; and because elsewhere there is a chapter devoted to the vagaries of mud banks, fast-flowing tides, and other maritime hazards, we will assume that there is a neighbouring stretch of gently-curving river devoid of such snags.

The winding curves of the river mean that some sections of
it will have the wind blowing across them, others will consist
of a stretch where the wind and the river are in line.   Clearly
your effort to sail along it for any distance will mean succes-
sive alterations of course, in which the simple evolutions of
tacking, reaching and running have each a useful function to

perform. There is no need to re-iterate these processes. The approach of the bank will make it clear that the course must be altered to avoid a nonsense. The only demand made on the helmsman, therefore, is to keep alive to the wind direction as you curve your course first this way and then that; for when sailing, *any* change of course means a fresh adjustment of the mainsheet to meet the new direction of the wind. Always keep the boat sailing; for unless the boat is moving through the water, the rudder has no flow of water past its surface, and so ceases to function. The drawings show better than words how running, then tacking, gives way imperceptibly once more to reaching. Then homewards once more by reaching, running and finally tacking back to the starting point. So far the dinghy has sailed half a mile down the river and back again without setbacks, and pride is swelling within. Beware. This is the moment when fate strikes most cruelly. On the last tack, just before going about to head back to the starting post, there is a sudden grating noise, magnified to alarming proportions by the sound-box effect of the hull; or perhaps even more sinister, the dinghy just stops dead without a sound. Surprise, surprise. In either case you are aground. The lowest point of the centreboard is jammed firmly on the bottom, whether of rattling shingle or soft embracing mud.

If your reactions are as swift as those of a cobra, and instantly the helm is pushed down to leeward, it is just possible to start the swing sufficiently to get the dinghy's bow round with the wind blowing it off shore, towards the deeper water whence you have just come. In this case a slight lift to the centreboard, and like a shopbreaker who has disposed of his half-brick at the moment of apprehension, you sail innocently back into the centre of the river. On the mud? Good heavens no—just pausing to think.

Suppose that occurs which is much more likely, and you fail to detach yourself. It is little use struggling to raise the centreboard. All this will do is to release the dinghy, allowing it to sail still further towards the shore, when both you and it will shortly come to a halt once more.

The cure for this predicament is as follows. The moment the dinghy stops, release the mainsheet. Then take an oar, and either push (if the bottom is firm) or paddle the bow of the dinghy round towards the wind, so that it faces finally back towards the channel. The purpose is to turn the dinghy through the same angle as it passes through when it goes about normally. As soon as the bow is safely through the

eye of the wind, and the sail begins to fill on the offshore tack, she is out of trouble. Lift the centreboard, and she will sail herself off.

The most difficult position to escape from, whether just after launching a dinghy or merely sailing aground in it by ill-chance, is that on a lee shore. This means that the wind is blowing straight on to the shore where you are, and it is useless to think that you will succeed in sailing off. The boat cannot gather way to tack until both centreboard and rudder are down; and if centreboard and rudder are down the boat is promptly aground.

Lower the sail promptly. Get out the oars, pull up the

centreboard and rudder, and row straight out to windward, well clear of the shoal water. There your best plan will be to find a mooring or another boat to make fast to while re-setting sail, stowing oars, and generally preparing to start afresh. Whatever the choice, first get well clear of the shore.

So far we have conjured up conveniently placed posts from which, like a fledgling bird, we have tried out our talents with only an occasional belly-flop. Posts are useful, for if you miss them or hit them, it doesn't really matter, and they are easier to grab than a mooring buoy.

However, a jetty is less accommodating and if, as is certain, you wish sooner or later to come alongside one, or another boat, it is important to do so gently, without damage.

Now a jetty or a boat may be pointing in any direction relative to the wind, so first distinguish on which side of it the wind is blowing; which is the windward side, and which the leeward, for it is always the leeward side you must go to. The jetty or boat will then provide some shelter, because it interposes between the dinghy and the wind; and the sail, instead of blowing her hard on to the jetty or boat and pinning her there, can, by easing the mainsheet, be progressively spilt of its wind on approach; until the boat's way through the water has been almost stopped on arrival. Never, never, with a fair wind under sail, run down to a jetty (or a buoy or a post) and hope to stop yourself like John Gilpin, by grabbing something as you rush past. If compelled to sail downwind to a jetty, as you might be for instance when sailing into a very narrow creek which leaves no room to round up head to wind alongside, then lower the sail well beforehand and blow in under bare poles. Or if this is impossible, head for a steep mud bank, sail the boat into it, and lower sail at leisure.

Exactly the same rule holds good for any approach to the lee shore we discussed earlier. The boat's speed must be brought down to the minimum, and this is just not possible as long as sail is set. Otherwise you may hole her on an underwater obstruction, or jam stones in the centreboard case. There is a strange prejudice abroad which seems to discourage one's blowing about in a dinghy under bare poles, but in fact it will steer very well down-wind, under good control, and at a speed which fits very well with the requirement above. Moreover it permits the adoption

of a lofty air of detachment from progress as it concerns lesser sailors, all of whom are arched double or straining like mad, while you are drifting along peacefully as if in the remoter stretches of the Shropshire and Union Canal, with time and a lifetime to spare. Ignore the puzzled glances you may provoke. Time is clearly your servant, for once, and you are rightly the envy of all who see you.

Chapter 4

TIDES

'Tides are queer things' said Davies, as if in defence of some not very respectable aquaintances. *Riddle of the Sands*.

THE middle of the Atlantic, or the Pacific, is going very slowly up and down. It has been doing this for years, and it really does not matter why. The part of this performance that affects us is that the slow wave wells up as it meets the shoaling waters of the coast, where its vertical movement is slowly translated into a horizontal one, causing the tidal stream which flows into our rivers for about six hours, and then ebbs out again for the next six. The process is inexorable, and inexhaustible, but by no means as frustrating as people would have one believe. The crux of the matter is to see that, as far as possible, wherever you go the tidal stream is on your side, or at least not opposing you.

The reason why it is so important to discover the tide's activities is that sometimes in the middle of a channel its speed may approach, or in light winds, even exceed that of your boat. This eventuality accounts for the remarkable sight you may see of people apparently sailing backwards. This is not the result of some successful research into a nautical Black Art. It just means at that particular point in

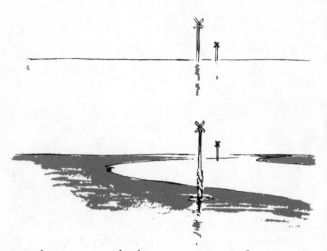

the river the contrary tide they are meeting is flowing out faster than they are sailing in. Manifestly they are being prevented from going where they wish, and sometime this is going to hold good for you.

Similarly when standing on the shore you may see sometimes a boat sailing briskly and normally through the water but at what appears to be a wholly unaccountable speed. The houses and trees behind it zipp past with a velocity more reminiscent of an early silent film. This is accounted for quite simply by the fact that the boat is having added to its speed the velocity of a fine fair tidal stream.

From all this, it will be seen that the tide business can have a profound effect on your sailing; and that is not the end of it. While the stream ebbs and flows to assist or delay progress, the tide also rises and falls to effect profound changes in the shape and area of navigable water. The fine stretch, for example, of Padstow or Chichester harbours as seen at high

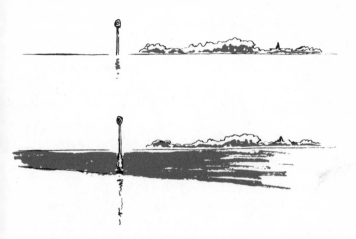

water, with blue sea stretching away for miles, will be changed by the ebb in a matter of hours into a complicated series of dry banks of sand and mud glowing in the sun, and if you haven't taken good note of what is going on, you too will be glowing, high and dry on top of one of them.

It is for this reason that in the early chapters on sailing I suggested expressly that the first sorties afloat should be made in non-tidal water, for at that stage of experience there was ample food for thought and observation in the effects and changes in the wind.

The streams, again for reasons that don't matter here, vary in their speed from week to week. They range from high speed, or *Spring* tides, which rise very high and sink very low, down to *Neap* tides about a week later, wherein their speeds are more sober and their rise and fall less dramatic. To enable you to forecast the state of the tides, sailing people have recourse to a yearly almanac which appears in many

different forms and if it is at all possible I should recommend that your early voyages, if they take place in tidal waters, should be confined as far as possible to the 3–4 days of neap tides; or if that is not possible, choose the early part of the flood spring tide, and the last two hours of it which precede high water. The reasons are (*a*) with a flood tide, if you go aground in a major way, the rising tide will float you off; and (*b*) that at high water spring tides there is water to sail a dinghy over very wide areas of most harbours. Ebbs flow more strongly than the floods and spring ebbs fastest of all, so at first you should avoid that period altogether.

Tidal streams, while they make no marked difference to sailing a boat in open water, have a profound effect on the rules of coming alongside jetties or picking up a mooring buoy. These articles are attached firmly to Mother Earth. The tide, like Old Father Thames, is rolling on to, or perhaps from, the mighty sea, and the tide, like the wind, can be your brake; it can also be your accelerator, and anybody knows the importance of keeping them distinct in your mind.

Before this new complication weighs too heavily, take comfort from the fact that close to the shore-line, where you are likely to launch your boat, or beach it, the flow is usually very slight and may often be ignored. Only when approaching or leaving a jetty which sticks out well into the channel is

it normally necessary to foretell and make provision for the tide.

The rough guides to action are these:

1. When wind and tide are coming from the same direction, luff head to wind to come alongside, or to pick up a mooring.
2. When the wind is blowing across the tide, make your

approach heading *into* the tide, and progressively slow the boat down by spilling the wind from the sail as you draw near.

3. It is when wind and tide are in opposite directions, that the operation of coming alongside or picking up a mooring becomes difficult, more particularly with a single-sailed craft. The essential feature is to approach against the tide, and to get the mainsail down just before grappling the jetty. If it is left set, full of wind and devil, it will keep the boat sailing full tilt, and you will be left stretched taut like a mediaeval plotter on the rack, trying to hold on, while the boat does its best both to climb on to the jetty and to pull your fingers out by the roots. But, with the sail down, the windage of the boat and rigging is usually sufficient to blow it

along over the tide, and if the boat sets a jib, of course the problem is even easier. Leave the easily-handled jib hoisted, to tow you peacefully along for the last few yards, before lowering it at the last moment.

If by some mischance you do find yourself already along-side and for some reason unable to get the mainsail down, due to a jammed halyard or some such hazard, the devilment of the boat will be quickly subdued by pulling up the centre-board and rudder, for it is the resistance of these two surfaces which keep the boat pinned round across the wind. As soon as they are removed the dish-like bottom of the dinghy loses its grip on the water, and she will lie head-on, or nearly head-on to the wind, enabling the sail to be lowered in peace.

While sailing out in the middle of the channel, clear of all obstructions and in the full force of the tidal stream, makes no particular demand on one's thoughts, a certain amount of

guile must be brought to bear if the stream is both strong and contrary, more particularly if the wind is light. It may well be, if beating against a foul tide in a failing breeze, that on each tack the margin of advance is growing smaller, and smaller, and smaller. That post with a supercilious cormorant on top was exactly opposite the last time you went about. The ·dinghy may be bubbling along splendidly through the water, but the fact is, relative to the land, she has stopped, and the cormorant knows it if you don't. .That is why he looks so supercilious.

Now is the time for guile. It will be noticed that the tide flows less strongly towards the two sides of the river. More than that, if the shoreline projects here and there, close by are areas of water which are clearly eddying back *upstream*. A series of short tacks therefore, close to one shore not only will escape the full force of the tide in the centre of the channel; they will take the dinghy into these areas of favourable eddy. Suddenly you will find that you have fooled that cormorant, and that he and his wretched post have dropped astern.

Like most unexpected windfalls of good fortune, there is usually some snag, so this time it should hardly be a surprise if you pay for your temerity by touching the mud on the inshore tack. Never mind, if all is ready, with one hand on the centreboard tackle, only a second will elapse as it is whisked up the necessary few inches to allow the dinghy to go about and tack back into deeper water.

If you are the fortunate possessor of a fair wind, but a strong foul tide is unfairly removing this advantage, the dinghy may be sailed similarly close along the bank to escape its strength, but pull the centreboard halfway up both to allow a closer approach, and to act as a sentinel if you tend to cheat too much and so touch the bottom.

Two final warnings are needed about tides. The first concerns the point at which harbours join with the open sea, often at a bottleneck a mere hundred yards or so across, through which there has to flow maybe the entire contents of a large inland harbour or river. These places should be treated with the greatest respect and I adjure you to keep well clear of them in every circumstance until you have been sailing for some considerable while. Not only is the speed of the tide often great, but it will result in a short, confused and angry sea, unsuitable for a small open boat in the hands of a beginner.

The second warning concerns boats and yachts moored in a tideway. When sailing in such a place it is important to remember that if the tide is flowing strongly, relative to the dinghy they are all under way, steaming along against the tide. It would not normally be considered safe to shave close across the bows of a boat under way and exactly the same rule applies here. In such circumstances, whether the wind is light or strong, keep well away from the bow of a moored boat, and if you have any doubt of your ability to do so, bear away and go under her stern.

Chapter 5

DEFINITIONS

I is my view that the copious list of nautical terms often pressed upon the beginner must be a most discouraging barrier to his progress, and if not enjoyment. Bear up, bear away, up helm, put the helm up, hard-up the helm, put the helm a-weather, all are meant to carry the same message; and that's just a start. 'Port your helm and luff her to windward of that hermaphrodite brig that's in irons'—this sort of stuff shouted in a loud voice is all very well, but it makes sailing much more difficult than it need be; and I suspect that those who insist on imposing it on the person who has only just grasped the bar of wood that steers the boat are being no help at all. In any case don't tell me that the proud owner of a newly-acquired dinghy is going to start his life afloat by sitting down on the sea wall to an intensive morning's study of Falconer's *Dictionary of the Marine*. Not a bit; he will clamber aboard his craft, use his common sense to see which rope needs pulling to set the sail, off he goes, and good luck to him. He does not know his port garboard from his mast sheave and it would not help him a bit if he did.

However, after a while he will begin to get interested in the bits that go to make his boat. He will find himself comparing her with other boats, and discussing points of

detail with other owners. Similarly he will find himself wanting to describe his activities under sail, or to ask questions relating to manoeuvres either of his own boat, or those of others. This is the moment to start collecting a marine repertoire, when the phrases can be related to something that is already familiar, but which have so far lacked a name.

Certain phrases concerning direction are immediately useful. *Ahead* and *astern* are self evident. *On the bow* means

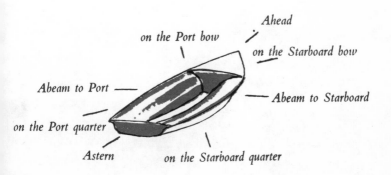

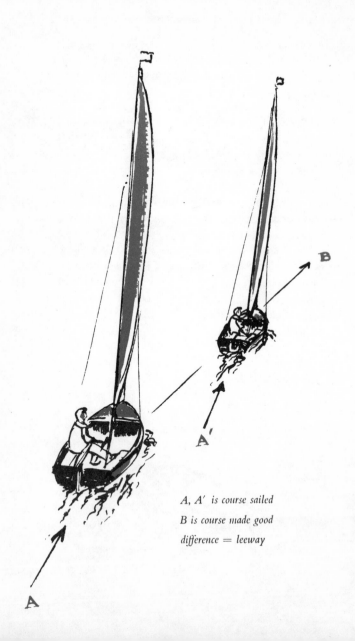

A, A′ is course sailed
B is course made good
difference = leeway

to one side or the other of the bow, *starboard* (right) or *port* (left) as the case may be, further round is the starboard or port *beam*, and finally to starboard or port *quarter*.

To windward, refers to the direction from which the wind is coming; to leeward means the exact opposite. So we get the windward side of the boat, where the helmsman normally sits, and the leeward side, over which he empties the bailer. *Leeway* is the angle between where a boat is pointing, and where she actually sails. *Missing stays* is when the boat loses way halfway through going about, and falls back on the original tack.

To steer a boat under sail with a tiller means that any alteration of course must be connected with the wind. To push the tiller towards the sail, and so turn the bow towards the wind, is to *luff*. The opposite, to turn the bow away from the wind, is to *bear away*. *Steady as she goes* or *steady* means maintain the course as at present. A *luffing breeze* is one which, due to a slight change in its direction, allows you to sail a rather more windward course than before. A *foul puff* is a flaw in the breeze which heads you off from your chosen course.

Here is a simple list of sea terms (by no means exhaustive) but so sited in the book that it stands a chance of being read. If it proves too indigestible at this point, it will still be here later on for reference purposes, meanwhile jump to p. 68.

Aback   Wind on wrong side of sails
Aft   Towards or beyond the stern
Abeam   At right angles to boat's fore and aft line
About, go   Tack or turn round through wind
Ahead   In front
Amidship   Middle of boat
Astern   Behind

Athwart Across boat

Ballast Weight to counterbalance force of wind in sails (in a dinghy this is the helmsman)

Bar Shoal water at entrance of river or harbour

Battens Thin strips of wood or plastics inserted into pockets in the sail to preserve its shape

Beacon Navigational mark

Beam Width of boat

Bear away Turn from direction of wind (opposite to *luff up*)

Bear off Push off

Beat to windward Act of sailing or tacking in direction of wind

Bermudan rig Jib-headed mainsail

Bight The slack in a rope

Bilge Where side of boat meets bottom

Block Pulley

Bollard Post of metal or wood for mooring

Boltrope Ropes sewn to edges of sails

Boom Spar at bottom of sail

Bottom Underwater part of vessel

Bow Front of boat

Broad reach Point of sailing with wind on or just abaft beam

Buoy Either navigational mark or mark for mooring

Burgee Triangular flag often bearing device of club

By the lee Running with wind blowing from the same side as that on which the sail is set

Cable One tenth of nautical mile (200 yds) or Anchor chain

Carry away Break

Carvel Hull built with smooth exterior

Centreboard Plate or fin lowered through keel to provide lateral resistance when sailing

Chain plate   Fitting to attach standing rigging to hull
Check   Ease off
Chine, hard   Angle of bilge
Cleat   Device for securing ropes
Clew   Forward bottom corner of any sail
Clinker   Hull built with planks overlapping
Close hauled   Sailing as near to wind direction as possible
Coaming   Board to keep out water e.g. cockpit coaming
Counter   Stern overhang of yacht's hull
Cringle   Eyelet in sail
Current   Horizontal movement of water other than that caused by tide
Cutter   Single mast rig with two headsails

Dinghy   Small sailing boat or tender to yacht
Dipping lug   Sail which is 'dipped' or moved round mast when tacking
Displacement   Weight of water displaced by yacht (i.e. the weight of yacht)
Down helm   Put tiller to leeward
Draft   Maximum depth of vessel under water
Drop keel   See *Centreboard*

Ebb tide   Fall of tide from high water
Ebb stream   Movement of water caused by fall of tide
Eddy   Local variation of current or tidal stream
Ensign   National flag of ship

Fairway   Navigable channel
Fathom   Measurement of depth of water—6 feet
Fenders   Cushions to protect sides of vessel
Fetch   To reach
Flood   Movement of water from low to high tide
Flood stream   Movement of water caused by rise of tide

Flow   Curve in sail

Foot   Lower edge of sail

Foresail, headsail   Sail set ahead of the mast

Forestay   Fixed stay from stem to masthead

Gaff   Spar at top of mainsail (when gaff rigged)

Gale   Wind force 8 or over, Beaufort scale

Garboard strake   Lowest plank next to keel

Gather way   Beginning to move through water

Gear   All the tackle of a boat

Go about   Tack. Turn through direction of wind

Goose winged   Running with main over one side and foresail held out over the other

Gudgeon   Part of hinge of rudder, see also *pintle*

Gunter lug   Triangular mainsail extended above mast by a gaff

Gunwhale   Upper part of boat's side

Gybe   Change of sail from one side to the other when running

Halyard   Rope (or wire) for pulling up any sail (or flag)

Hank   Metal or plastics device for fastening luff of headsail to stay

Harden-in   Pull in (sails)

Head   Top corner of sail

Headboard   Board sewn into top of sail

Headsail: Foresail   Sail forward of the mast

Heel   Boat—lean over. Mast—foot or bottom

Helm   Tiller or steering wheel; 'up' move tiller to windward, 'down' move tiller to leeward

Hitch   Method of making fast e.g., to post (not a knot)

Home   'Sheeted' home. Pulled in taut

Horse   Bar or wire across stern along which main sheet moves from side to side

Irons, in Head to wind and unable to pay off on either tack

Jib Foremost headsail (in a cutter)

Kapok Buoyant vegetable fibre used for life jackets
Kedge Small anchor
Keel Lowest part of hull
Ketch Two-masted sailing vessel. Mizzen mast is stepped forward of sternpost
Knees Wooden or metal supports in boat's frame (under thwarts, etc.)
Knot Measurement of speed (e.g. speed 5 knots = 5 nautical m.p.h.)

Laid-up Unrigged. Dismantled
Lanyard Several turns of line used to tauten shrouds Knife/whistle lanyard
Lash To tie to
Leach Rear edge of sail
Lee Side away from wind
Leeboard Like a centreboard but hung on ship's side
Leeward To the lee
Leeway Angle between direction in which boat points and actual course, i.e. wind blows boat a little sideways in spite of lateral resistance of keel or centreboard
Leg A tack
Let draw Allow sail to fill, e.g. on new tack
Let fly Let go suddenly
Limbers Holes in frames of boat to allow water to flow
Loom Handle of oar
Luff Forward edge of sail
Luff up Sail closer to wind
Lug Quadrilateral sail (see drawings)

Mainsail   Principal sail of boat
Marline   Light two-strand tarred line (string)
Marlinspike   Tool for splicing rope
Mast step   Socket into which heel of mast fits
Miss stays   Fail to go about
Mizzen   Sail on after mast in yawl or ketch
Mooring   Heavy weight(s) or anchor(s) to which vessel lies permanently.
Moulded   Hull made by glueing together thin strips of wood in or on a mould

Navigation   The art of taking a vessel from one point to another.   (Purists will restrict this to trans-ocean movement)
Neap tides   Period of small tides

Offing   Make offing; get away from (shore)
On the wind   Close hauled
Overfall   Steep waves caused by tidal stream
Overhaul   Gain on (sailing).   Free a rope or chain

Painter   Rope attached to bow of boat for making her fast
Pay off   Boat's head swings away from wind
Pennant, Pendant   Long triangular flag.   Part of rigging
Pintle   Inserting part of hinge of rudder
Point   Angle, one thirty-second part of a circle, i.e. 11 deg 15 min. Point of a compass: north, etc.
Points: (reef)   Short lanyards on either side of sail for tying up reef
Port   Left hand side facing forward
Port tack   Sailing with wind blowing on port side
Pram   Boat with flat bow
Purchase   System of blocks and rope to increase mechanical advantage

Quarter   Sector between beam and stern

Race   Disturbed water, e.g. where two tides meet
Rake   Angle made by mast in fore and aft direction
Range   Of tide, distance between low and high water
Reach   Angle of sailing between On the Wind and Wind Abeam
Reef   Shorten sail
Ride   Vessel rides at anchor or mooring
Rig   Arrangement of masts and sails
Rigging   Running rigging for controlling sails. Standing rigging for supporting mast
Rigging screws   For adjusting tension of standing rigging
Roach   Curved edge of sail
Roll   Motion of boat from side to side
Rowlock   Pronounced rollock. Fulcrum or crutch for oar
Rudder   Flat board or plate hinged to stern for steering
Running   Sailing with the wind abaft the beam
Running rigging   See Rigging

Scantlings   Dimensions of parts of vessel
Schooner   Two-masted rig with mainsail aft
Seize   Fasten together by lashing
Set up   Adjust correctly (usually rigging)
Shackle   D-shaped device for connecting rigging, e.g. for fastening sheets to foresail
Sheave   Grooved roller in block
Sheets   Running rigging (ropes) for controlling sails
Ship   Take on board, e.g. water
Shroud   Stays for mast athwart boat
Single part   Without purchase, e.g. sheet or halyard
Slack off (*away*).   Let out
Slack (*water*)   When stream is stationary (e.g. between tides)

Sloop   Single masted rig with one headsail
Snub   To stop suddenly
Sound   To find depth of water (to take a sounding)
Spar   Metal or wood pole for setting a sail
Spinnaker   Special sail for running before the wind
Splice   To join rope by interweaving strands
Spreader   Strut to improve efficiency of rigging
Springs   Very high or low tides
Stand on   To maintain course and speed
Starboard   Right hand side looking forward
Starboard tack   Sailing with wind blowing on starboard side
Stem   Vertical timber forming framework of bow of boat
Step   To put in position, e.g. mast
Stern   Back of boat
Sternway   Movement stern first
Sternpost   Aftermost vertical timber of framework
Strake   Plank

Tabling   Reinforcement of sail—seam round edge
Tack   Foremost bottom corner of sail
Tack   Sail (beat) to windward close hauled with wind first on one side then on other.   To alter course through the wind.   A leg of the course when beating to windward. See *Port Tack*.   *Starboard Tack*
Tackle   See *Purchase*
Take charge   Get out of control
Thwarts   Seats across boat
Tidal stream   Horizontal movement of sea caused by tides
Tide   Vertical movement of sea due to Solar and Lunar attraction
Tide-rode   Vessel at anchor lying head to tide (especially in contrast to *wind-rode*)
Timbers   Framework of yacht (ribs)

Tingle Metal over fabric patch used to stop a leak
Tonnage Measurement of capacity (size) of vessel
Topsail Sail set above gaff mainsail in fore and aft rig
Transom Square stern of vessel

Unbend Untie
Under way Moving through the water (N.B.—not 'under *weigh*')
Unship To remove
Up helm An order to move tiller to windward

Warp Rope used for anchoring or securing vessel to mooring or quay
Warp (to) Move a vessel by hauling on ropes
Waterline Horizontal length of boat where it rests on water
Waterlogged Floating, but full of water
Way Movement through water
Weather (side) Windward side
Weigh (to) Raise the anchor
Well Cockpit
Whip To bind the end of a rope to prevent it unravelling
White horses Breaking tops of waves
Wind-rode When vessels at anchor lie head to wind (especially in contrast to *tide-rode*)
Withy Small tree, stake or perch to mark the channel in a creek

Yacht Vessel used for pleasure
Yaw To swing from side to side of course
Yawl Two-masted rig with small mizzen mast which is stepped aft of sternpost
Young flood First slow movement of flood stream

1. *Gunwale*
2. *Bilge rubber*
3. *Keel*
4. *Stemhead*
5. *Garboard strake*
6. *Top or Sheer strake*
7. *Rubbing strake*

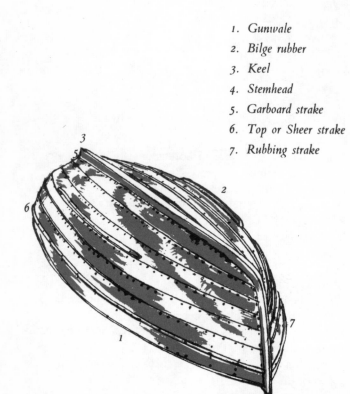

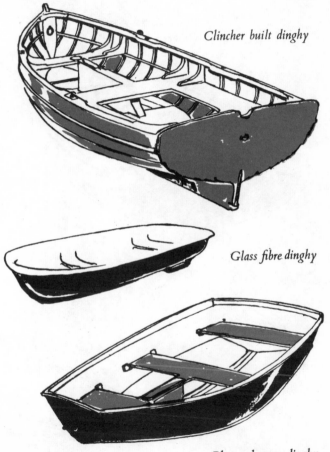

Clincher built dinghy

Glass fibre dinghy

Plywood pram dinghy

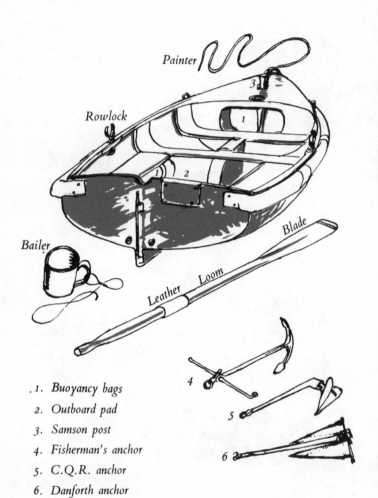

Painter

Rowlock

Samson post (3)

Buoyancy bags (1)

Outboard pad (2)

Bailer

Leather Loom

Blade

1. Buoyancy bags
2. Outboard pad
3. Samson post
4. Fisherman's anchor
5. C.Q.R. anchor
6. Danforth anchor

Some useful knots

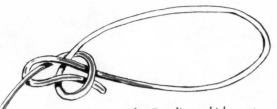

The Bowline *which creates an eye of a fixed size in the end of a rope for making fast dinghies, or for putting over a bollard*

The Figure of Eight, *a stopper knot to prevent the end of a rope escaping through a block*

The Clove Hitch, *for attaching a rope to a post, or for the end of a shroud, lanyard, etc.; it may jam tight when wet*

Sheet Bend *for joining together two ropes of unequal size*

Knotting and Splicing is a craft well worth extensive study, for there is a wide variety of different types for different purposes

1. *Reef taken by tying reef points*

2. *Reef taken by roller-boom*

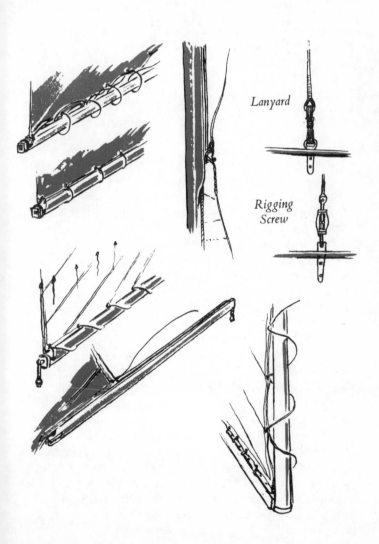

Lanyard

Rigging Screw

Chapter 6

BUOYANCY AND SAFETY

IDEALLY, every dinghy sailor can swim. Though capsizes are uncommon except in racing fleets, they do occur, and people get drowned. The ironical fact is that they are sometimes drowned *because* they can swim. All too often this is how it happens.

First of all a dinghy out in a fresh breeze is sailed away from other craft, perhaps two or three miles out into the open sea. It is a fine day, and the sun is shining as she bounces along from crest to crest, her well-equipped crew rejoicing in her speed. Suddenly somebody's foot slips, or perhaps the boat falls off the crest of a wave; anyway something unplanned occurs, and over she goes. From being just visible as a tiny white triangle on the horizon, she is now invisible. The crew is competent and well supplied with supporting buoyancy, as is the boat, but every time they are just about to succeed in righting her, an extra large sea rolls her over once more. So far there is nothing to worry about except to stick by the boat and keep trying, but after a while one of the crew begins to lose some of his strength, and a degree of concern arises. Would it not be better for A, who is a very powerful swimmer, to set off for the shore? It might be, but to exercise his powers to the full he'd better get rid of this hampering life jacket, so off he goes, and that is the last time A is seen alive. Meanwhile the remainder hang on, supported by their buoyancy and in no particular distress, until some hours later a passing boat spots them and their troubles are over.

Not one, but two, absolutely vital lessons are illustrated here. The first is that no open boat should be sailed in open water out of easy sighting-distance of other craft. No matter how confident you feel in yourself and your boat, and how set fair is the weather, it is asking for trouble. Others have done it, and will do it, but don't you.

The second lesson is this. NEVER leave your boat in the hope of swimming ashore. Your boat is a source of support and possibly shelter, and is far more easily seen than a single head in the water. You are far more likely to survive, if it comes to that, by sticking to the ship.

After all that, the question may be posed as to why is it so necessary, with personal buoyancy and so on, for someone to be able to swim? The answer is that a non-swimmer is like a log in the water, and should he be swept a few feet away from the boat, he cannot even regain it. Quite apart from this, the swimmer on or in the water is at once at home with this element. On it, or in it, like the Water Rat, it's all the same to him.

Buoyancy is not the only subject which needs discussion

in this context.   Every sailing dinghy, naturally, should have
built-in buoyancy disposed both fore-and-aft in the hull, so
that when full of water it floats with the gunwhales above the
surface.   This buoyancy can be supplied by inflated bags
lashed firmly into place with webbing or by sealed compart-
ments integral in the construction of the hull; both systems
should be inspected periodially to see that they are, in fact, as
airtight as they seem.   A buoyancy bag may be only half-full
of air, yet still bulge convincingly.   An unsuspected knock
may break the air-seal of a buoyancy compartment in a
manner which only reveals itself when inspected closely.

There is no need to go to the extreme of capsizing the boat
in order to lose things overboard, though a capsize clearly
gives everything the best chance of gently floating away out
of your reach.   The simple answer is to tie them up like so
many mountain goats.   Lanyards should be spliced to every
moveable object, bailer, rowlocks and so on, so that they are
safely tethered; for example, at one time and another a young
fortune in bailers must have been committed to the deep,
and it is too late to remember the lanyard as the wretched
thing circles solemnly into the depths beneath your nose.
Incidentally, it would be a mistake to grab one of those natty
little bilge pumps with the idea that it is useful for emptying
a dinghy you have just filled up to the thwarts.   What you
want then is a good-sized bucket, with, of course, a lanyard
on its handle.

The oars should be stowed by tucking them under the
centre thwart, whence they cannot escape, but where they
can be withdrawn easily for use if need be.

Spare clothes, or food, or thermos flasks, or fishing lines,
or skin-diving paraphernalia, or dark-glasses, or cameras, or
grandfather's gold watch . . . well, anything you decide
to take with you sailing needs putting in a waterproof bag

of some sort and securing in a safe place. It is no use being beguiled by the magnificence of the weather into thinking that the near-calm in which you are currently drifting along will remain unchangingly thus all day. A smart little breeze against the tide will be splashing spray into a boat almost before you know what is happening, and by then everything has fallen into the lee bilge in a heap, and what isn't wet with spray from above is quietly absorbing all the bilge water it can from underneath. Incidentally, if the boat has no locker forward, the driest patch is usually right aft, just underneath the tiller, where you may confidently stow your bank-roll, if you have one, knowing that it will be safe from everything except a capsize. But preferably leave all valuables ashore; they are out of place in an open boat.

Chapter 7

PILOTAGE

THIS impressive-sounding affair is not what it sounds. It does not involve hiring a local man of infinite wisdom to pilot the dinghy safely through the multiple hazards of his harbour.   It is far more fun than that, and might be likened to the intelligent use of a road map to find your way past ☒ near ▮ (avoiding the pitfalls of *PH* (Inn) to the ⬭ where the heather is in full flower.

The prime difference between pilotage afloat and map-reading ashore is that the sailor has many more deductions to make from very much less evidence.   It is at once a fascinating and skilful art.

It may be thought that the extent to which it will affect a beginner in a dinghy can only be small, but from the moment that he lets go the painter on his first trip he will be carrying out an exercise in pilotage, and so it will continue as long as he shall sail.   For instance, at this minute, and requiring an immediate answer, you must know in what direction you can safely sail.   Does one pass to the left or right of that upright pole, sticking out of the water, topped with what might well be a rusty upturned paint can?   What does it mark?   Is it the end of a private jetty that is concealed beneath the ruffled surface of this very high spring tide?   And, by the way, what time is high water?   Because if you don't know, you ought to have found out, as at high water spring tides the sea will cover all the sandbanks, and will make it difficult to see the whereabouts of the channel.

These pin-prick questions of gadfly-doubt need cause little concern at this moment; they are posed merely to show how necessary it is to have the answers. In practice, one may manage to bumble around busy anchorages without getting into bother, but in the early stage of apprenticeship it is obviously better to find a clear patch of water which is devoid of snags both above and below the surface, leaving one free to concentrate on the matter of learning to sail.

Even so, the learning stage should not be used as a reason for ignoring surroundings as they appear on the local chart. Quite the reverse; it is a fascinating discovery to see how a scene already familiar appears to the hydrographer, and it is an important part of the equipment of a pilot to absorb this range of experience as soon as possible. The chart may well become superfluous quite soon in an often used area, but it is certain that one will go progressively further afield as time goes on, and may well visit entirely new harbours where familiarity with charts is essential.

On arrival in a new coast one should ask questions of local people (there is nothing so flatteringly effective as asking questions) about the local conditions. Produce the chart and get them to point out the various features marked on it (though you may take with a pinch of salt any claims that a particular harbour is uniquely difficult. It isn't true). Mark (in pencil, not ink) anything of major importance, so that when sailing about and with no spare hand for the chart, such points may be kept in mind.

The piece of chart reproduced will give an idea of what to expect, but I urge strongly the acquisition of the largest possible scale chart of the chosen sailing district before going afloat for the first time, and study it both at home and on the spot as soon as possible. Bits of history peep out from most of them; they are full of interest but need familiarity to provide of their best.

So far we have described and illustrated pilotage purely as it concerns navigating safely over a fixed seascape and its features, the buoys that must be left this side, or that; the leading marks that must be brought into line to guide craft safely through the deep water channel, and the sandbank that awaits the inattentive dreamer who forgets to pay attention to their silent message. Nowadays, however, the waterways and estuaries are dotted with moving craft of one sort and another, and these too must be avoided, for

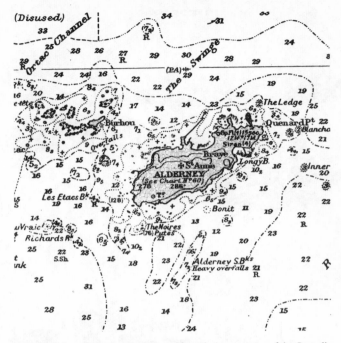

Reproduced from Admiralty Chart No. 2669 with the permission of the Controller
of H.M. Stationery Office and of the Hydrographer of the Navy.

collision with another moving boat is likely to involve far more damage than a casual grounding episode. To avoid them there is devised the seaman's Rule of the Road, of which the following is a basic extract.

RULE OF THE ROAD AT SEA

Two Sailing Vessels meeting (Rule 17). When each has the wind on a different side, the vessel with the wind on the port side keeps out of the way of the other vessel.

When both have the wind on the same side, the vessel which is to windward keeps out of the way of the vessel to leeward.

Note: This rule is expected to come into force sometime in 1966. Until then the following rules will be observed: A vessel running free shall keep out of the way of a vessel close-hauled. A vessel close-hauled on the PORT tack keeps out of the way of a vessel close-hauled on the STARBOARD tack. Both vessels running free with wind on different sides, the vessel with the wind on the PORT side keeps out of the way.

When both vessels are running free the windward vessel keeps out of the way of the leeward one.

A vessel with the wind aft gives way to one close-hauled.

Two steamers meeting (Rule 18). Head on. Each shall alter course to *Starboard*.

Two steamers crossing (Rule 19). The vessel which has the other on her starboard side shall keep out of the way.

Steam and Sailing vessels (Rule 20). The steamer shall keep out of the way, *except in restricted waters*.

Vessels to keep course and speed (Rule 21). The vessel with right of way shall keep her course and speed.

Vessels to avoid crossing ahead (Rule 22). Any vessel which has to keep out of the way of another should, if possible, avoid crossing ahead, and should, if necessary, reduce speed, stop, or go astern (Rule 23).

Vessels overtaking (Rule 24). Shall keep out of the way of an overtaking vessel.

Vessels in narrow channels (Rule 25). Every steamer shall, when it is safe and practicable, keep to that side of the fairway or mid-channel which lies on her starboard side.

Sailing vessels to avoid fishing vessels (Rule 26).   Vessels under way shall keep out of the way of vessels or boats fishing with nets, or lines, or trawls.

Special circumstances (Rule 27).   In obeying and construing these rules, due regard shall be held to all dangers of navigation and collision, and to any special circumstances which may render a departure from the above rules necessary to avoid immediate danger.

If an approaching steamer gives a signal on her siren or fog horn, and if no other boat is near, probably the signal is directed at you.   The officer of the watch or the pilot is telling you what he intends to do.

SOUND SIGNALS

Rule 28.   1 short blast; altering course to starboard.
2 short blasts; altering course to port
3 short blasts; my engines are going astern.

A steamer with right of way, doubtful if the other vessel will alter course, may give 5 short whistle blasts, but this does not relieve her obligations under Rule 27.

If everybody knew, and executed the above directions, life afloat would be much easier than it is.   Unfortunately, and it is no use blinking the fact, they don't.   So many people who drive cars have never bothered to find out that when they come afloat the Highway Code should be left on the beach; and there are a few others who, one suspects, care not for the Highway Code ashore, nor any other code of conduct wherever they may be.   All this makes pilotage difficult. There must be added the occasions when boats are racing (a fact notified by the square racing flags they fly) and it behoves everyone not competing to do their best to keep clear. Fortunately, just when your faith in the system is beginning to waver, some vessel approaches which both knows and applies the Rule of the Road at sea, when the whole thing begins to make sense once more.

Naturally there are occasions when common sense dictates some course of action not specifically dealt with by the Rules. Suppose when sailing slowly across a narrow waterway, a distant merchant ship is seen approaching.   Do not, at this early stage of experience, wait to see if she will pass well clear, even if you feel confident that she will.   Put the helm over immediately; gybe, go about, but whatever it is, do it soon, so that the pilot on the bridge of that vessel is able to dismiss you entirely from his mind and concentrate once more on the difficult task he has to perform.   Similarly, if confronted by an active group of boats, maybe manoeuvring prior to a race, or a cavalcade of yachts all by chance charging down a fairway in a bunch, steer clear, even if you have technical right of way.   To exert claims on one craft may start off a chain reaction among the others, and the final result may be to provoke a collision which need never have happened.

To determine whether, in fact, what the Rules call 'risk of collision exists', there is a useful test which can be applied very simply.   If a vessel approaching appears constantly in the same direction (or on the same 'relative bearing', say in line with the dinghy's rigging) then there is risk of collision.   The diagram makes this clear.   The earlier this fact is appreciated the better, for it permits an early decision about who holds right of way, and therefore which vessel has the duty of altering course.   If you decide that the other vessel has right of way, alter course boldly and in plenty of time, so that the other helmsman is left in no doubt of your intentions. In the case of a yacht which you suspect may be using power as well as sail, play for safety by treating her as being solely under sail. Yachts under sail can travel at a surprising speed even in light weather, and even an expert may find it hard to distinguish the facts.

Part of pilotage under sail is concerned with keeping control of craft in difficult or complicated conditions, wherein much

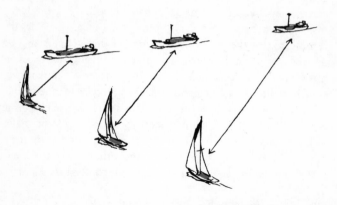

of the skill comes from anticipating events.

All buildings, moored craft, trees or quay walls cast a *wind-shadow*—that is to say, they will interrupt the free flow of the true wind, and inasmuch as one voluntarily takes shelter from a strong wind by standing close to some large object, so the passage of a dinghy into a sheltered lee will have the same result. The dinghy loses the wind, and stops; more-over it can take a tediously long time to escape from this

If in doubt — ' When the boom is on the right, get out of the light '

position, a fact often made painfully clear by the swift passing of other craft whose helmsmen have shown guile by passing clear to leeward, where the breeze is still blowing briskly.

Again, on warm calm days in a broad estuary, it will sometimes be noticed that a light breeze will be blowing all along one shore, but nowhere else. If one can but reach those thin, dark blue lines which denote a draught of wind on the surface, a gentle sail of several miles may follow, but failure to detect its presence means a prolonged and fruitless drift.

It sometimes happens that the wind-shadow of an obstruction not only cuts off the true breeze, but produces an eddy which strikes the sail afresh from the lee side, seldom with much force, but with disconcerting suddenness. Again, when passing once more clear of the wind-shadow into the true breeze, one may meet a puff of wind much stronger than the average wind-speed, usually caused by the funnelling effect of the obstruction to windward.

Naturally, when under way a certain amount of advance information can be gleaned by knowing what to look for. The changing direction of smoke from a chimney ashore denoting the coming of a wind-shift; the swing of moored boats announcing the turn of the tide; the flurry of disturbed water and fussy wavecrests that betoken shoal water, or the meeting of two tidal streams. In time one comes to absorb and act upon such signals unconsciously, in the same way that one steers a car or bicycle with unconscious accuracy, placing it naturally to suit changing conditions.

Occasionally it will happen that a beat up a river is so conditioned by the wind direction that one *leg* is nearly at right angles to the line of advance, while the other heads directly, or almost directly along the channel. If the tide or current is contrary, this up-channel leg should be steered most heedfully, for by luffing sufficiently the lee-bow of the boat is presented to the tide, and the resultant *course made good* is highly advantageous, the boat being pushed bodily to windward in a most satisfactory and useful way.

In a different context, but in logical sequence to a piece of pilotage, when the broad sandy beach, that looked-for haven, is finally reached; when the dog has stopped trying to bury the picnic basket, and the valiant helmsman is ensconced on the dunes with a bottle of beer, it is an unwelcome discovery to notice that the wind will persist in blowing the dinghy on to the shore instead of allowing it to lie off, where it will float despite the falling tide. This tiresomeness may be cured either by leading the painter round a shroud, and lashing the rudder to steer the boat offshore; or alternatively,

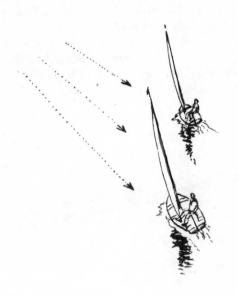

and (more satisfactorily) by balancing the anchor and cable on the foredeck, all clear as for letting go. A long piece of light line is attached to the crown of the anchor. Give the boat a good shove offshore, and as it reaches the limit of its progress a sharp tug on the light line tips the anchor overboard in deep water, and the dinghy lies moored off, allowing the helmsman to return to his bottle of beer, and to what the dog has left of his lunch.

Finally, there is a golden rule for amateur pilots in strange waters. *Caveat emptor*—or beware of the empty space. If in a broad haven yachts or craft are moored in a long sinuous series of curves, it is certain that there lies the channel; the sunlit areas of water which stretch away on either hand to the distant tree-lined banks are nothing but a shallow snare. If you look carefully you might even see a gull paddling knee deep (if a gull has knees) where you would otherwise suppose there to be ample depth of water for you to sail. Be warned; a gull only draws two inches, and in any case, unlike you, has feet designed for soft mud.

Chapter 8

WEATHER

THE subject of the weather is a huge one, and for all the knowledge we possess of what causes its changes, there is no escape from the fact that it never stops fooling us. It may well be asked, in that case, what on earth is the use of writing about it. Well, I am not writing of the passage across continents of occluded fronts and their global effects—instead the subjects are just you and your dinghy, out for a sail together.

There was a Naval Admiral, whose name is scarcely less well-known than Nelson's, called Beaufort, and the wind that is blowing gently across the water was classified by him as Force 1. He describes it as a light air, 1–3 knots in speed, causing 'the formation of ripples with the appearance of scales, but without foam crests, and sufficient to give good steerage way to fishing smacks with the wind free'. Under its influence the dinghy will be sliding along quietly and steadily on any point of sailing, but Admiral Beaufort is not always so tranquil, and his higher numbers are like anything but this. However, what is needed at present is the prudent limit of wind strength in which to sail safely. The criteria I suggest are those of a different kind. If halyards of boats and dinghies are tapping relentlessly; if moored boats are heeling in a cross-wind; if the leaves of trees are in more

Beaufort Number	Limits of Wind Speed in Knots	Descriptive Terms	Sea Criterion	Probable Height of Waves in ft
0	Less than 1	Calm	Sea like a mirror.	—
1	1–3	Light air	Ripples with the appearance of scales are formed but without foam.	$\left\{\begin{array}{l} \frac{1}{4} \\ \frac{1}{2} \end{array}\right.$
2	4–6	Light breeze	Small wavelets, still short but more pronounced. Crests have a glassy appearance and do not break.	
3	7–10	Gentle breeze	Large wavelets. Crests begin to break. Foam of glassy appearance. Perhaps scattered white horses.	2
4	11–16	Moderate breeze	Small waves, becoming longer: fairly frequent white horses.	3½
5	17–21	Fresh breeze	Moderate waves, taking a more pronounced long form; many white horses are formed. (Chance of some spray.)	6
6	22–27	Strong breeze	Large waves begin to form; the white foam crests are more extensive everywhere. (Probably some spray.)	9½
7	28–33	Near gale	Sea heaps up and white foam from the breaking waves begins to be blown in streaks along the direction of the wind.	13½
8	34–40	Gale	Moderately high waves of greater length; edges of crests begin to break into spindrift. The foam is blown in well-marked streaks along the direction of the wind.	18
9	41–47	Strong gale	High waves. Dense streaks of foam along the direction of the wind. Crests of waves begin to topple, tumble and roll over. Spray may affect visibility.	23
10	48–55	Storm	Very high waves with long over-hanging crests. The resulting foam in great patches is blown in dense white streaks along the direction of the wind. On the whole the surface of the sea takes a white appearance. The tumbling of the sea becomes heavy and shock-like. Visibility affected.	29
11	56–63	Violent storm	Exceptionally high waves. (Small and medium-sized ships might be for a time lost to view behind the waves.) The sea is completely covered with long white patches of foam lying along the direction of the wind. Everywhere the edges are blown into froth. Visibility affected.	37
12	64+	Hurricane	The air is filled with foam and spray. Sea completely white with driving spray; visibility very seriously affected.	

than gentle motion; or if tall grasses are bending to the
breeze, then there is considerably more wind than you are
ready for—yet. In the early stages of learning it is undesir-
able that a dinghy should need 'sitting out', and that is what
these indications imply.

So much for the wind as it is. What of its future
behaviour? It is not much use listening to a weather forecast
on the wireless, except as a rough guide to major trends. In
such a specialised sense local conditions can vary widely
both over wind strength and direction. In general, whatever
the surface condition, it is wise to suspect the weather when

High hills produce squalls

clouds are hard edged, and moving fast overhead. Similarly,
rain and overcast conditions with a SE or southerly wind are
both harbingers of worse to come. If venturing far from
shelter (and in these conditions I advise against it) be ready to
turn for home early—not that it will be necessary to stop
sailing, for this is not the case. There are many areas near the

top of rivers and estuaries where the shelter is such that you may sail comfortably during the presence of strong winds outside. What must be guarded against then are the puffs and squalls which from time to time penetrate the gaps in the trees or hills. An approaching puff is easily seen by the dark line it makes by ruffling water, and its threat is much less if the helmsman is prepared for it, ready to ease or let go the sheet but realise that he is naturally looking ahead, and the squall is more than likely to come from some different direction, abeam or, maybe on the quarter, to jump on him unaware.

Remember too, unsettled weather requires not only alertness, but also agility, for the stability of a dinghy relies a good deal on the weight of the crew moving to windward, counterbalancing the pressure of the sail. I have known it happen in a puff of wind, that a sort of hypnotic paralysis assails the inexperienced helmsman of a dinghy.

So used is he by now to grasping the mainsheet, that when the moment comes to let it slip to spill some of the wind

from the sail, and to ease the tiller to allow the dinghy round up towards the wind, his faculties desert him. Grimly, as in a trance, he holds on. The gunwale goes down; the dinghy is roaring along. He can't even bring himself to shift his weight on to the gunwale as a counterbalance. Fortunately most dinghies seem stiff enough to survive this treatment; the squall eases, up she comes, and everyone breathes again. Remember, always, that if in a strong squall both tiller and mainsheet are released completely, a dinghy will look after itself quite happily, forging slowly ahead, almost upright, the sail making a prodigious noise and there is nothing whatsoever to worry about. If you feel as though things are getting out of hand, just drop the sail and row up to the shelter of the weather shore. There are no medals given for getting into a knot, and doing so isn't likely to teach anything useful. Should the dinghy ground in such circumstances on a lee shore, lower the sail promptly; up centreboard and rudder, and let the boat blow ashore, where she can be pulled up and there is time to get your breath back. If the prospect of a capsize is worrying, take an early chance on a fine day of deliberately capsizing, both to check the effectiveness of the system of tying things into the boat, and to practice righting the boat. Having tipped the boat over, and yourself into the water, first lower the sail, then swim round and bear down on the centreplate. Should it have fallen back into its slot, any rope attached amidships can be used to roll the boat over. Both the speed at which she comes up, and the rate at which a bucket empties her out, will be a surprise. In doing this, climb aboard only over the transom, and unless the centreboard opening is above water, the slot *must* be blocked with a sweater or piece of sail before starting to bail.

Winds cause waves; big winds cause big waves. Tides

opposed to winds cause the most obstreperous waves of all. A beat into a stretch of a mere half-mile of river where a moderate breeze is blowing against a strong tide, will find short breaking crests everywhere, and the dinghy thumps and flings the spray about.

There is nothing at which to be alarmed, for a large amount of spray, accumulated over quite a period, say 20 minutes (which may seem a long while) still only amounts to a few inches of water in the lee bilge. Nevertheless if the boat, and you, are getting damper than circumstances warrant, veering a little mainsheet and sailing her more upright and more slowly, will leave the tide to take her to windward. It is not good practice, incidentally, to try to escape the spray

Not this —   *or this*

over the weather bow by moving progressively aft. Dinghies are extremely sensitive to trim, or in other words the disposition of weight, and it is perfectly possible to make the best-designed dinghy sit down and sulk, miss stays, and commit many other atrocities by putting the crew's weight other than somewhere near the midship point.

Chapter 9

STRUCTURE, RIGS AND SAILS

Until a few years ago the general pattern of building boats had not altered greatly since Noah launched the Ark. The principle is not unlike that of the spine and rib-cage of a human being, and the art of the shipwright in joining together the hundreds of pieces so that they form a strong watertight whole is, to me, one of everlasting wonder. There is barely a straight line anywhere, and each curved piece of wood has to be met thoroughout its course by another curved piece which fits precisely and snugly. No other craftsman in wood works in such a remarkable way to build something that is so severely treated in use, and to a large extent keel-yachts are still constructed in this traditional system.

Small boats and dinghies, however, have been the subject of many structural experiments in recent years. The invention of plywood, and the process of moulding two or more layers into a smooth curved surface have revolutionised the industry. Here the chemist has taken charge, as he also has in the materials devised for ropes and sails.

Three typical cross-sections of plywood and moulded boats are illustrated. The chief advantage of this type is the simplicity of mass construction (many types are suitable for amateurs to build) and the lightness of the finished boat.

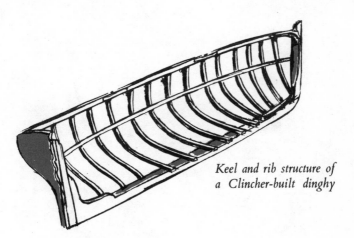

*Keel and rib structure of
a Clincher-built dinghy*

Cross-section of above

Another, and important, point is that most of these boats are properly and carefully designed by an expert, so that a beginner almost certainly can find out a great deal about existing boats before committing himself to buy one. All

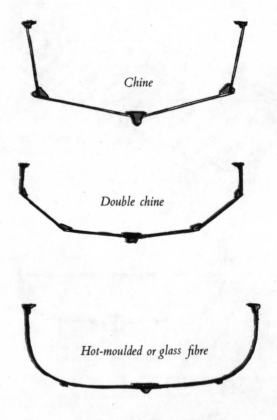

Typical hull sections

such craft have a variety of good qualities; it is just a matter of discovering which has what.

The rough differences between a good traditional type and a modern boat are these. The modern dinghy sails better, is lighter, and is easier to maintain; but it is more susceptible to damage and scars, and these are less easy to rectify without the scars being apparent; it is also, due to its lightness, less inherently stable under sail. This statement may be regarded as mildly controversial, but I believe it to be true, and in any case I don't suggest that a modern boat is unstable, merely that it will need 'sitting out' rather earlier as the breeze comes up.

Rigging is divided into two sorts. Standing rigging, which, as its name implies, is permanent and supports the

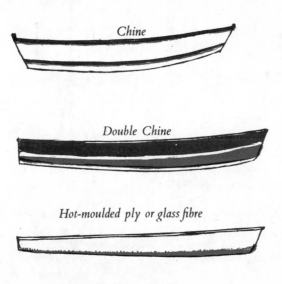

Chine

Double Chine

Hot-moulded ply or glass fibre

Modern dinghy construction

spars; and running, which hoists the sails and trims them to the wind. The simplest of rigs, with which we have sailed in the early stages is already familiar. Shown here are the common varieties seen in small boats and yachts, together with their names.

Sails today are largely made of Terylene, a material whose indifference to damp and mildew has brought about its

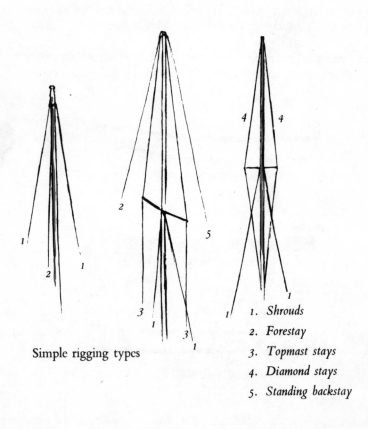

Simple rigging types

1. *Shrouds*
2. *Forestay*
3. *Topmast stays*
4. *Diamond stays*
5. *Standing backstay*

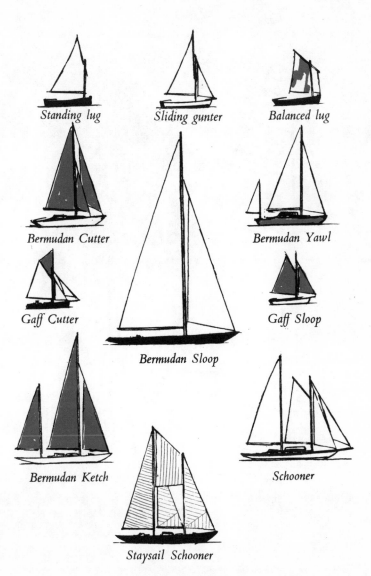

Standing lug

Sliding gunter

Balanced lug

Bermudan Cutter

Bermudan Yawl

Gaff Cutter

Gaff Sloop

Bermudan Sloop

Bermudan Ketch

Schooner

Staysail Schooner

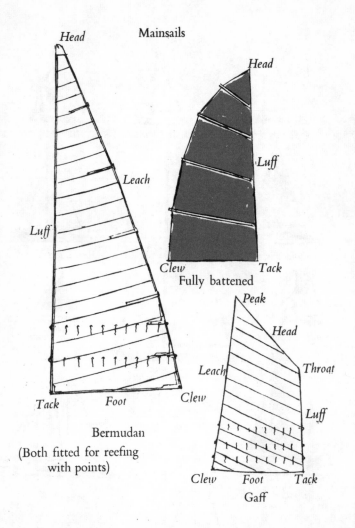

Mainsails

Head

Head

Luff

Leach

Luff

Clew   Tack
Fully battened

Peak

Head

Leach   Throat

Luff

Tack   Foot   Clew

Bermudan
(Both fitted for reefing
with points)

Clew   Foot   Tack
Gaff

Headsails

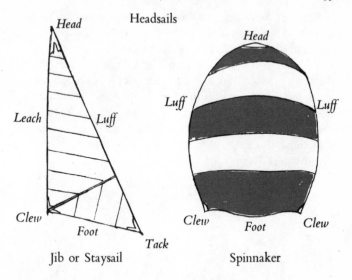

Jib or Staysail   Spinnaker

replacement of cotton. The drawback to cotton is its capacity to absorb moisture and to shrink. This means a perpetual round of care to see that it is not forced out of shape, that it is stowed only when dry, for the successful 'flow' in a sail is easily upset by distortion and this is almost impossible to rectify. Sails should set smoothly, without wrinkles, and the edges should neither curl nor flap, for a flapping edge (a common fault often cured by inserting battens) shakes the whole sail and upsets its flow. Setting a dinghy sail does not require prodigies of effort—(it is absurd to apply the same force to 50 square feet as you would to 500) and when it is set and full of wind it is easy to see whether you have hit off the right degree of tension. You will find, however, that ordinary rope halyards (as distinct from Terylene rope or wire halyards) tend to stretch under tension, and may need setting up again after a short while under way.

Because the waters frequented by a beginner are almost
certain to accommodate yachts and motor boats of every
size and description, I have illustrated a variety of these
craft under way, for the sake of the interest and information
they can provide.   Watching other people is no bad way to
learn, indeed some claim that the cheapest and best illustrated
lessons are those provided by other people, so I have added
some comments which, in a perfectly harmless sense, may do
something to explain why these boats behave as they do in
their owners' hands.

*This traditional type of vessel is not easily handled in confined waters, so
keep clear*

Fast motor cruisers are apt to leave a heavy wash and are sometimes ignorant of the problems of sail

Racing buoys are often the focus of converging craft, all of which are in a hurry

Craft manœuvring under reduced sail need plenty of space

Craft under tow should be avoided

Dinghies before a start are quite unpredictable, so keep clear

Chapter 10

CARE OF A BOAT

I⊤ is a gloomy reflection that any artifact, boat, car, house or what-you-will, is in a state of decline from the moment of its completion, a comment which might be said to include most human institutions—but certaiŋ it is that boats, if neglected, age very quickly; but on the more cheerful side is the fact that properly looked after they preserve wonderfully well. Beside this, nothing is so rewarding to the owner as the effect of maintenance on his craft.

The first rule of wood is that left bare of paint and varnish it loses its colour, and weathers very rapidly. The resulting labour of restoration is out of all proportion to the neglect that has taken place, and there is no escape from it, particularly with transparent varnish work. The second rule of wood is that salt water is relatively harmless stuff—in fact salt has such preservative qualities that the old coasting schooners had the air spaces round the hull packed with salt; it is fresh-water, allowed to lodge in joins and to lie there for weeks and months on end that is the killer.

To reduce unnecessary wear and tear try to keep your boat where the shore traffic is least; where joyous children do not jump blithely in and out of her when she is high and dry, to grind the paint off the bottom, and the varnish off the thwarts and bottom boards. Eschew the social jostle of dinghies on a hard, across which other people clamber on their way to the pub; and back. Take out anything moveable, lest it disappear overnight. And as soon as you see a patch of paint rubbed bare, or a chafe beginning, do rub it down with sandpaper and retouch immediately. It is of

Types and use of fenders

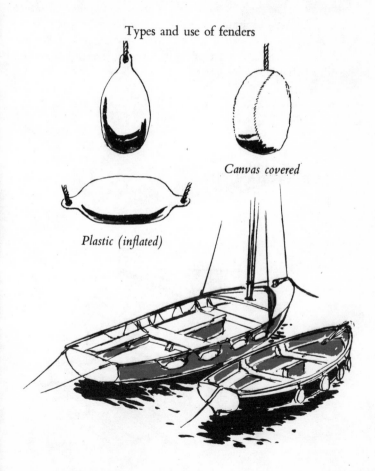

Canvas covered

Plastic (inflated)

course heart-rending to have a boat's pristine sides scarred the day after painting them, but these things happen, and apart from relieving your immediate feelings, it is no use, no use at all, starting to curse; the author of this outrage is probably 150 miles away by now, and entirely indifferent anyway. The only thing to do is to put it right, starting immediately, and using materials designed for the job.

The lightness and structure of a plywood dinghy makes it suitable for hauling out clear of the water, preferably on a trolley. If it is to be left for any length of time it should

either be covered with a canvas awning, or turned upside down and raised a few inches on baulks of wood. Sails which have got wet in salt water should be taken home, hosed down and hung up to dry. Spars should be suspended by at least three points; taking care to see that no 'set' or curve occurs, for once this develops there is no remedy. Shackles, rigging, screws and blocks need lubrication from time to time with a water repellent grease.

If an open boat has to be left afloat on a mooring, either arrangements will be needed to have it bailed out from time to time, or, better than this, get an awning which will lash down all round the coaming to keep out the rain. Lacing it on every time you leave the boat may be a nuisance but it means peace of mind, and preserves the varnish work from the rays of the sun. The mooring, if possible, should be clear of other boat traffic, and made of chain or wire, rather

than rope. Not unless the dinghy is of a racing type will you need to bother about the chance of it being capsized by a strong gust of wind during a gale, in which case some previous arrangements with the local boatman or club will be necessary.

Kept afloat, a boat will tend to get foul with weed which grows on the bottom with amazing speed in fine weather, and while the first whiskers round the waterline do not affect the boat's performance, the general appearance suffers as in a 'before' and 'after' shaving advertisement. Thereafter it is more than looks which suffer, and a really foul boat is heart-breaking to sail. Frequent scrubbing or the use of anti-fouling paint will keep the weed in check, and these chores are by no means a hardship in a small boat—in fact there is no better fun than sailing down to a nice sandy beach on a hot day, equipped with scrubber and bucket, to play a legitimised grown-up version of buckets and spades, with trousers rolled up to the knee and sand squirting up blissfully between the toes.

Apart from the effect on the eye of all these chores and pleasures of maintenance, there is the very practical point that a neglected boat, in a competitive market, will be hard to sell; and if, as seems likely, you wish to finance part of your next purchase on the price you get for this, the moral is clear. Look after your boat and in turn it will look after you.

Chapter 11

TRAILERS, CLOTHES AND LIFEJACKETS

I SUPPOSE as many as half the dinghies of today cover many more miles towed on a trailer than they do on the sea. This requires special equipment. It is not only useless but dangerous to suppose that any lash-up will suffice. The ball-joint attached to the car must be securely bolted to a properly designed bracket attached to the chassis, not the bumper, and the trailer itself must be designed for the job, providing strong clamps to hold the dinghy in place both vertically and horizontally. If the trailer is to be used both for towing and launching, it is important to see that its wheel bearings are of the sealed type, indifferent to being ducked in salt water and sand, which together will encompass a destructive and speedy end to any other variety. In addition there are questions of registration plates, rear-lights, and perhaps most important of all, appropriate insurance. Having once watched an escaping dinghy mast on a towed trailer scarify harmless shoppers like the scythes on Boadicea's chariot, there must loom large the risk of compensating an angry queue of avaricious dependants.

There is, of course, a variety of trailers on the market, one of which is the most appropriate choice for your boat, and the way you will be using her. Choose one built by an established manufacturer, for though it will cost a little more,

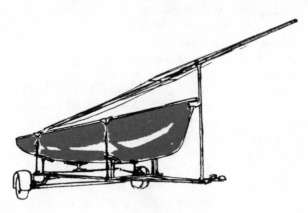

Ready for the road

it will cause no anxiety on roads which grow daily more complicated and congested, and where there is trouble enough without a dinghy taking charge unexpectedly.

The appropriate clothes for sailing a small boat are a matter of personal taste, as well as practicability. It is only in the last twenty years or so that, led on by the resourceful designs of war-time special equipment, clothing manufacturers have attacked the problem (mostly concerned with keeping dry) in earnest. Until then people tended to regard getting soaked as an inevitable consequence of sailing, and indeed if this prospect is regarded with peculiar abhorrence it might be better to stick to halma for a pastime. The fact is that under certain circumstances it is almost impossible to keep entirely dry—the question is merely how much of you is going to get wet. There is no collar to an oilskin jacket that will keep out water—a towel is the only answer. Long oilskin coats are clumsy, hampering articles in a small sailing dinghy. Choose the coat and trousers variety, and resign yourself to wet feet, whether or not you decide to wear shoes. Rubber boots are to be discouraged, even when they are of such ample size that they can easily be kicked off, for when filled with water, as in a capsize, they are a hampering nuisance, if not downright dangerous.

If you have the misfortune to capsize, and are unable for one reason or another to right the boat, do not be tempted to start casting off clothes. Your buoyancy will see to it that you remain afloat, and the clothes that you are wearing will tend to retain a small layer of water round the body, the temperature of which is slightly higher than that of the sea.

Mindful that choice of clothes is supposed to reveal one's personality, an observation that must arouse interesting speculations at some yachting centres, it is not necessary, despite the foregoing, to equip yourself for the starting platform of a Cowes club in order to sail a 12 foot dinghy. It is part of the clothing manufacturers' success to persuade people to buy his products, and in the early stages, when encounters with mud and weed-bestrewn painters are commonplace, I think it better to spend money on one's boat than on getting dressed to sail it. Above all eschew a yachting cap; few articles can be so inappropriate for a beginner in a dinghy, where the errant boom will certainly whisk it into the sea. Apart from this, such headgear implies (though by no means guarantees) a degree of expertise, so the wearer may find himself called upon to know all the answers.

Far more important, in my view, than the variety of clothes *de rigeur*, is the knife on a lanyard, a knife which is sharp, and provided with a spike; and the buoyancy jacket. Lifejackets have come under such close scrutiny in recent times that one can be bemused by the rival claimants to notice, whose several voices have created deafening confusion. Clearly there is room for a personal decision here, but a good yardstick is the British Standards Specification. A life jacket should therefore bear the B.S.I. 'Kitemark', and when acquired, should be worn, not left tucked in the stern locker until so many things are happening that it is too late to put it on. It should also be examined carefully from time to time, to see that no harm has come to the fabric or material on which its buoyancy relies.

So now, equipped with dinghy, and a cheerful determination to master the sailing of it, the moment has come to push off. Good luck, good sailing, and remember the advice of that great sailor Slocum: 'To face the elements is, to be sure, no light matter when the sea is in its grandest mood. You must then know the sea, and know that you know it, and not forget that it was made to be sailed over'.

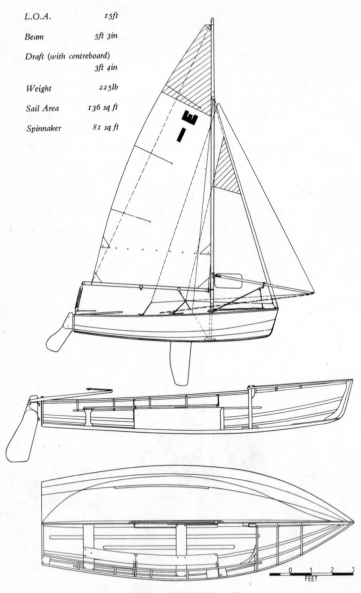

L.O.A.	15ft
Beam	5ft 3in
Draft (with centreboard)	
	3ft 4in
Weight	225lb
Sail Area	136 sq ft
Spinnaker	81 sq ft

'Yachting World' Lazy E

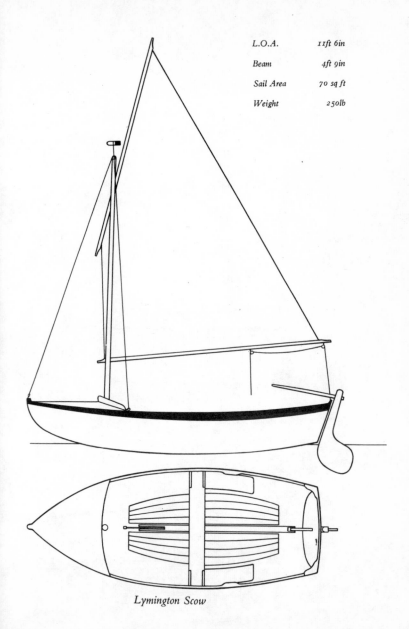

L.O.A.	11ft 6in
Beam	4ft 9in
Sail Area	70 sq ft
Weight	250lb

Lymington Scow

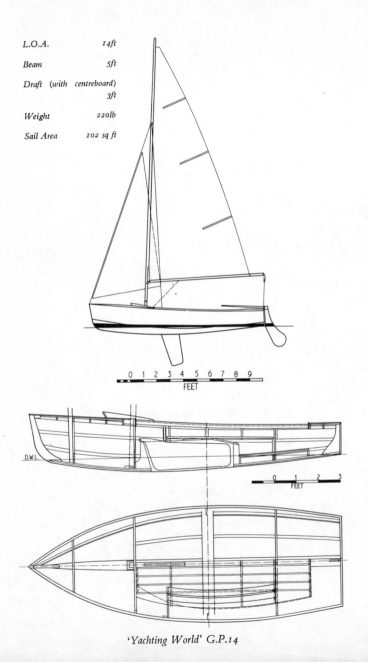

L.O.A.	*14ft*
Beam	*5ft*
Draft (with centreboard)	
	3ft
Weight	*220lb*
Sail Area	*102 sq ft*

0 1 2 3 4 5 6 7 8 9
FEET

D.W.L

0 1 2 3
FEET

'Yachting World' G.P.14

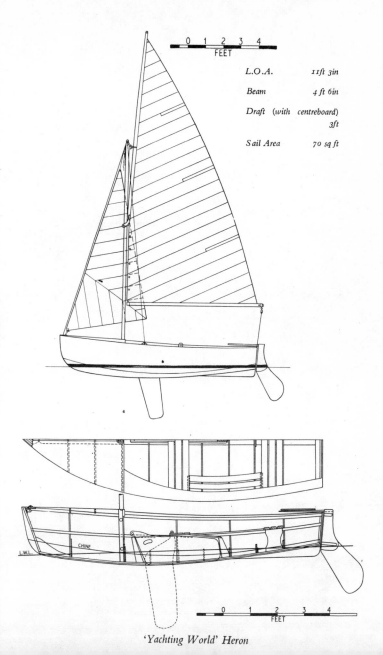

L.O.A.   *11ft 3in*

Beam   *4 ft 6in*

Draft (with centreboard)   *3ft*

Sail Area   *70 sq ft*

FEET

CHINE

L.W.L.

FEET

'Yachting World' Heron

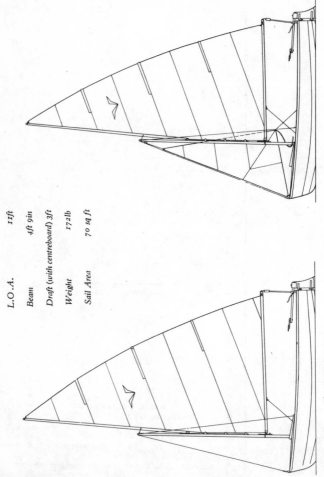

L.O.A.	11ft
Beam	4ft 9in
Draft (with centreboard) 3ft	
Weight	172lb
Sail Area	70 sq ft

Alternative Rig